The Bugle's
DICKTIONARY

Unabridged, unadulterated,
unflattering, unconcise edition

EDITED BY ANDREW PEGLER
ILLUSTRATED BY SELDON HUNT

The Bugle's Dicktionary is proudly brought you by www.buglecorp.com The Surgeon General advises that seatbelts must be worn when reading and advises against use in case of fire. *The Bugle's Dicktionary* was tested on animals and is best served cold. Contributions for the next edition are welcomed via info@buglecorp.com

Published in 2004 by
Hardie Grant Books
12 Claremont Street
South Yarra, Victoria 3141, Australia
www.hardiegrant.com.au

All rights reserved. No part of this publication may be reproduced, stored in a retrieval system or transmitted in any form by any means, electronic, mechanical, photocopying, recording or otherwise, without the prior written permission of the publishers and copyright holders.

The moral right of the author has been asserted.

Copyright text © Andrew Pegler 2004

National Library of Australia Cataloguing-in-Publication Data:
Pegler, Andrew.
  The Bugle's dicktionary : unabridged, unadulterated,
  unflattering, unconcise edition.
  ISBN 1 74066 194 X.
  1. Australian wit and humor – Dictionaries. 2. Invective –
  Australia – Dictionaries. 3. Invective – Australia – Humor.
  4. Swearing – Australia – Dictionaries. 5. English
  language – Slang – Dictionaries. I. Title.
427.994

Cover and text design by PipandCo.
Illustrations by Seldon Hunt
Printed and bound in Australia by Griffin Books

10 9 8 7 6 5 4 3 2 1

Aa

Entries

beginning with the above
letter or character

about to find pups *adj*. Pregnant; shot in the giblets, *up the duff*.

acidue *n*. Small pieces of broken heart and other emotional debris that remain at the scene after an ugly breakup.

acluistic *adj*. To be without a clue; to have no idea whatsoever. Also *boofhead*; *fidiot*; brick with eyes.

acorn *n*. That little bell end from which tall oaks grow… when you *get wood*.

Admiral Browning *n*. Chocolate log; that which sinks the Bismarck. See also *schload*.

Adolf Hitler *golf term* To have 2 shots in the bunker.

Adrian *rhym. slang* Smashed; rhyming slang for Adrian Quist, famed Australian tennis player.

air biscuit *n*. Fart; botty burp. Floating body of trouser gas. As in 'Could you open a window? I think somebody has launched an air biscuit.'

air dirt *n*. A hanging plant in a bachelor flat.

air the orchid, to *v*. To beat around the bush; engage in *gusset typing*. (*Orchid* is also Greek for testicle.)

alcologic *n*. A fermented system of reasoning, this fuzzy logic is only understood with a *gutful of piss*.

Alice Springs *n*. The holiest of holies. The bit in the red centre.

angel *n.* Pillow biter; passive male homosexual.

apache *n.* 1. Sex without a condom; riding bareback. 2. Popular hit by sixties guitar combo The Shadows.

apeshit, to go *v.* To get very angry. As in 'Gooze found the esky empty and went apeshit at Wazza and Brownie'. See also *chuckin' a Dokic*.

Aphrodite's Evostick *n.* Semen; human bonding fluid.

arse *exclam.* A negative reply, expressing denial. As in 'Did you *cut my lunch*?' 'Did I arse!'

arse bandit *n.* He who breaks into another man's *Vegemite motorway*, or sheaths his pork sword in *barking spiders*. See also *crack haunter*.

arsecons *n.* Of information technology, those computer keyboard symbols used illustratively to indicate the condition of an arse. E.g. Normal arse (_!_) Lard arse (__!__) Tight arse (!) Sore arse (_*_) Slack arse (_o_).

arse-feta *n.* Inedible cheese matured in the narrow passage leading to *Cadbury Alley*.

arse grapes *n.* X-Piles; unwanted visitors from Uranus.

arseholed *adj.* Intoxicated; shitfaced; *rat-arsed*; blotto; having partaken in an excess of wallop.

arse into gear, to get one's *phr.* To stop being lazy, or to hurry up. As in 'Get your arse into gear, you toe-poking ferret!'.

arse-piss *n*. Diarrhoea; rusty water; anal firewater; Jap flag juice.

art pamphlet *n*. A jazz or scud magazine; one-handed reading material.

as rare as rocking horse shit *phr.* Rare.

as useless as *phr.* Underlines uselessness. As in 'As useless as a horny donkey in a bag of mice; tits on a bull; cheese in a bushfire; the pope's balls'.

at it *adj*. Engaged in copulation. The use of this term is restricted to disapproving neighbours. As in 'Tsk, sounds like those two next door are at it again'.

Aussie kiss *n*. Similar to French kiss but given down under. See also *great Australian bite*.

awaken the bacon, to *v*. Sexually arouse the male; stimulate the penis; polish the pork sword.

Bb

Entries
beginning with the above
letter or character

baby gravy *euph.* Semen; smegma. Also baby bullion.

baby's dinners (ba-*beez* di-*naz*) *n.* Breasts; tits; pink passion blancmanges.

back door Benny *euph.* A qualified *brown-pipe engineer*.

back door conquistador *n.* An hombre who wears a cocoa sombrero.

back flanker *rhym. slang Vic.* Wanker; tosser.

backseat driver *n.* 1. Car passenger who criticises the driving of another. 2. Gentleman who puts his *sixth gearstick* up the exhaust pipe of another.

backwards burp *n.* Fart; air dump; tree monkey.

bacon bazooka *n.* Penis; pork sword; pink oboe.

badly packed kebab *n.* *Gutted rabbit*; *hair pie*; hairy bridle. See also *mapatasi*.

bag *v.* To denigrate or bad mouth.

bagpipe *n.* Armpit sex; to ignore the pink and the brown, and shove the cue straight into the top corner pocket.

bald man *n.* The penis; Kojak; Captain Picard; *Spurt Newton*.

Ballarat *n.* A fully erect penis. As in 'Are you ready yet, Bruce?' 'Almost there, Sheila. I'm nearly at Ballarat.'

ball buster *n.*
Sexually aggressive female; cock chomper.

balls *n.* 1. Testicles; those spherical spunk factories on the Scrots Road Industrial Estate. 2. Courage; guts. As in 'I like him. He's got balls.' 3. *exclam.* Denial. As in 'Has he *balls* got balls!' 4. Rubbish; nonsense. As in 'Balls! Of course he's got balls.' 5. Egg-shaped things you play rugby/AFL with.

balls deep *adj.* A pork sword buried to the hilt; the maximum length with which it is possible to *slip someone* in a sausage and donut situation; the maximum extent to which the sausage can be hidden. See also *up to the apricots*.

baloney colonic *n.* A non-medical procedure not covered by Medicare where the baloney owner tries to sneak it through the back door. Front bum equivalent is to sweep with the *womb broom* or give the kidney a tickle.

baloobas *n.* Bazoomas; *norgs*. See also *headlamps*.

banana yoghurt *n.* Breakfast alternative to porridge, to either swallow or spit.

barkers' eggs *n.* Dog turd. Those things laid on the pavement. Also dog toffee.

barking spider *n.* Ringpiece; freckle; *chocolate starfish*; *ring*.

barnication *n.* The act of self-flagellation whilst mumbling distorted Scottish.

Barossa Valley *n.* Known for a big fruity mouth feel and long finish. Relating to sweet minge from South Australia. Similar palate to *Cunter Valley*. Always well bred, the fruits of the Barossa Valley are for the refined palate, often distinctively vanilla-laced, with a slightly fishy nose. See also *hairy chequebook*.

Barry Crocker *rhym. slang* A shocker. As in 'Mate, I am having an absolute Barry on the Dapto Dogs today'.

barse *n.* The perineum; that little bit between your balls and your arse. Also known as biffin bridge, stinkers bridge, chin rest, taint.

basket for days *phr.* Well hung; donkey-rigged; double-hung; hung like a bull; miracle meatworker.

bastard *n.* A footy umpire.

bats' wings *n.* Delicate alternative to *spider's legs*.

battered sav *n.* Saveloy in fanny batter, often with extra scrunchies.

batting for both sides *euph.* Bowling from both ends, as opposed to the pavilion end.

bearded blood sausage *n.* Blue-vein meatroll.

bearded clam *n.* Vagina; fanny. As in 'How did you get on, Bruce? Did you spear the bearded clam?'

bear trapper's hat *n*. Hairy front bottom. As in 'She had a fanny like a bear trapper's hat'. Also Davy Crockett's hat.

beaver leaver *n*. He who chooses to leave beaver in favour of cack pipe. A gentleman of the back room. See also *ring stinger*.

beer callipers *n*. Imaginary leg splints with which arsed stragglers make their way home from the pub after closing.

beer coat *n*. Invisible coat that keeps you warm for that long stumble home.

beer compass *n*. Inbuilt device that ensures your safe arrival home despite the fact you are so pissed you don't know where you live, how you got there and where you were a moment ago.

beer goggles *n*. Optical lenses that allow mutual attraction/ sexual activity between those who would ordinarily not be attracted. See also *beersightedness*.

beer scooter *n*. Mystical vehicle that ferries you home, like a magic carpet, without any recollection of it. As in 'I don't even remember getting home last night. I must have been picked up by the beer scooter.' See also *mystery bus*.

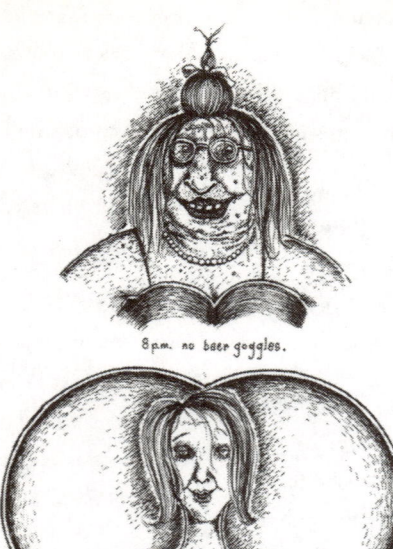

8 p.m. no beer goggles.

2 a.m. with beer goggles.

beer goggles *n.*

Optical lenses that allow mutual attraction/sexual activity between those who would ordinarily not be attracted. See also *beersightedness*.

beersightedness *n.* An eye condition that arrives quite suddenly after 'last call' in which members of the opposite sex appear more attractive than they were earlier. See also *beer goggles*.

bell *n.* Clitoris. As in 'You can ring my b-e-e-ell, ring my bell. Ding dong, ding dong'.

belly flopper *n.* A clumsy brown trout whose graceless entry into the water causes splashing of the arse.

belt-fed mortar *Army sim.* As in 'I bet she bangs like a belt-fed mortar.' Also shithouse door in the wind; *kangaroo-shagging space hopper*.

Benaud *n.* A particular shade of beige favoured by cricket commentators and cack-pipe engineers.

bender *n.* Prolonged drinking spree.

bend the elbow, to *v.* To go for a *beer goggles* fitting.

berko, to go *v.* To have a brain explosion; lose it; do ya nut. See also *chuckin' a Dokic*.

better than a *phr.* Underlines how good something is. As in 'Better than a poke in the eye with a burnt stick; bleeding mule sandwich; J'Lo's blind, nude, desperate twin sister on crack.'

bevvy *v.* & *n.* Booze; drink.

BHP Steel *n.* Serious wood; überbone.

big cock day *n.* A day, quite possibly in spring, the arrival of which is greeted with the *dawn horn* and throughout which the sap continues to rise. For example 'As he wrestled himself into his *grundies*, Darcy knew it was going to be a big cock day.' *(Pride and Prejudice by Jane Arseten)*.

big in the shitter *adj.* Someone whose arse looks like the side of a house. Often accompanied by a head like a *bulldog chewing oats*.

big white telephone *n.* Dunny.

bikini burger See *hairy pie*.

Billy Graham, a *phr.* Make a decision for Christ's sake. As in 'Gazza, we gonna get a slab of VB or a bottle a Bundy?' 'I dunno, Waz, Billy fucken Graham, mate!'

Billy Mill roundabout *n. UK* Climactic point of masturbation. From the end of A1058 coast road near Newcastle, UK. As in 'My mum walked in just as I was coming up to the Billy Mill roundabout'.

biscuits *n.* 1. *UK* Contents of the stomach after a heavy night's drinking. As in 'Get me a bucket, quick, I'm gonna chuck me biscuits'. 2. *US* Attractive buttocks.

bit *n.* Unspecified quantity of sex, usually partaken 'on the side'.

bitch piss *n.* Coolers, bottled Alcopops. Also drunk by men who complain about 'the dust in here'.

bitzer *n.* Mongrel dog.

Bjelke *n.* A pumpkin scone big enough to keep a whole state in suspended animation for decades.

blood fart *n.* As bad as it gets; deep trouble; up the shit.

blood nut *n.* A redhead.

bloody *adj.* The great Australian adjective.

blowie *n.* 1. A large, maggot-laden fly common in summer. See also *dunny budgie*. 2. *Head, good*; a blow job.

blue *n.* A human bingle; a fight. See also *umecarparknow*.

bluey *n.* 1. Favoured all-Aussie working dog. 2. Anyone with red hair.

BOBFOC *acronym* Body off Baywatch, face off Crime Watch. Best viewed in swimwear, with a bag over his/her head.

bog snorkelling *n. Dirtbox* (as opposed to *muff*) diving.

bogan *n.* Any individual living more than 100km from the coast who drives a 1983 Telstar and thinks the G spot is a nightclub in Frankston.

boint *n.* The after-meal tradition of smoking a joint with guests.

bogan *n.*
Any individual living more than 100km from the coast who drives a 1983 Telstar and thinks the G spot is a nightclub in Frankston.

bollocks *n.* 1. Nonsense; balls, as in 'That's utter bollocks, that is'. 2. Knackers; balls, as in 'Them's massive bollocks, them's is'.

bomb bay *n.* The arse; the area of one's body towards which the *rear gunner* is attracted.

Bondi cigar *n.* Floater; brown-eyed mullet.

bone *n.* Erect penis.

boofhead See *fidiot*.

Bourneville Boulevard *n. Arse; fudge tunnel.* Used to denote homosexuality, as in 'I believe he strolls down the Bourneville Boulevard'.

box brownie *n.* A variation on the very popular parlour game, *'hide the sausage'*, in which the owner of the sausage changes hiding bays from box to brownie.

box of assorted creams *n.* She who has recently been over-accommodating to a number of gentlemen; a promiscuous female with a fanny like a billposter's bucket.

box the Jesuit, to *v. 17th C.* How Robin Hood and his merry men would have referred to bashing the bishop.

Bradman, a *phr.* When the chance of getting a *bit* is 99.94% (the big man's average) i.e. very good, but not 100%. As in 'Jeez, Wazza was goin' gangbusters wif that chick last night. I wooda called a Bradman, if only 'e dinnit fall over and piss 'imself.'

brain cramp *n.* Condition where the brain and penis are locked in battle for control over the mind, leaving the talker with a 1000-mile stare. Compare *cunt-struck*.

brap *n.* The volume rating of a fart (Bp) governed by three variables: rectal pressure (r), buttock friction (f) and sprouts consumed (SpC).

$$Bp = r/f \times SpC$$

Buttock friction can be reduced to zero by pulling the ringpiece open wide during emission.

Brett Lee, a *n.* A sexual manoeuvre involving very fast balls aimed at the box down a good pitch on a wet day. Say no more.

brewer's daughter *n.* From Australian folklore. A mythical woman of unquestionable, almost impossible attractiveness. Fables also paint her as an exhibitionist and mad shagger.

brewer's droop *n.* Marshmallowing of the penis due to excessive alcohol intake. Fallout from a *hops hunger*.

brewer's fart *n.* A particularly strong smelling fart. As in 'Fuck me, he's just dropped a brewer's fart, grains and all'.

Brigitte Bardog *n.* Any horny old tart who's seen too much sun and with whom it is always your shout.

Brisbane *n.* A mythical place where Australian brains go to die.

Britney Spears *rhym. slang* Beer. As in 'Two Britneys please, Julie'.

brown-pipe engineer *n.* A plop plumber who always visits via the tradesman's entrance.

Bruce Lee *n.* Erect nipples; as hard as a nip. See also *docker's thumbs*.

brunner *rhym. slang* Do a runner. Compare *Rex Hunt*.

bucket arse *n.* Promiscuous and indiscriminating homosexual male. Much loved by the amphetamine-fuelled *one-eyed night crawlers in turtleneck sweaters*.

build a log cabin, to *v.* To pass an enormous stool. As in 'I wouldn't go in there mate. Someone's just built a log cabin.' Also U-blocker.

bulldog chewing a wasp, head like a *sim.* An ugly face. 'She had a face like a bulldog chewing a wasp.'

bulldog chewing oats *phr.* Post-coital vagina. As in "She had a fanny like a bulldog chewing oats.' Earliest recorded use in Shakespeare's *Henry IV*, act II. 'And lo, do I see that my ladies' bulldog hath been chewing oats again?' See also *cream biscuit*.

bulldog licking piss off a nettle, head like a *sim.* See *bulldog chewing a wasp*.

bum conkers *n.* See *arse grapes*.

bum gravy *n.* Diarrhoea; rusty water.

bung *adj.* Stuffed; fucked; bent out of shape; not working as it should; rooted.

bung hole *n.* Vagina. See *fizzing at the bung hole*.

bunny boiler *n.* A histrionic woman, unhinged, over-possessive. Often pain-in-the-arse princess type. From the rabbit-boiling scene in *Fatal Attraction*. As in 'Keep clear of that slapper, she's a deadset bunny boiler'.

burial at sea *n.* The dignified delivery of a stool, without splashback. Not a depth charge or *belly flopper*.

bury a quaker, to *v.* To dispense with the contents of one's rectum; crimp one off; release a payload from the *bomb bay*.

bushman's hanky, to use a *v.* To place one index finger on the outside of the nose and blow. See also *get out and walk*.

bush oyster *n.* Nose gravy.

butt nugget *n.* Smaller faecal nugget left hanging from the *paddo end* after the foresection has been crimped.

button broker *n.* Pimp; petticoat merchant; fishmonger.

butt slammer *n. derog.* Member of the gay community.

butt sneeze *n.* Fart.

Cc

Entries

beginning with the above
letter or character

cab sav *n.* *Head, good* in a taxi at the end of a messy night, after which the man may reciprocate by drinking at the *Barossa Valley*.

Cadbury Alley *n.* See *Bourneville Boulevard*.

camel's foot *n.* Of leggings and tight jeans, those mounds and crevices generated in a lady's crotch when they are pulled up too tight. Also known as camel toe, Twix lips and *badly packed kebab*.

can slaughter *n.* The act of murdering a tinny.

Captain Hogseye *n.* Curly-bearded seafarer with a shiny, bald, purple head who trawls in *cod cove* and spits a lot.

Captain Stabbin' *n.* He who is always on the job. Dirty dawg; mad rooter. More *toey* than a Roman sandal; hornier than a *dog with two dicks*. See also *fanny rat*.

carnival *n.* From extremely old jokes, a sexual position in which a woman sits on a man's face and he has to guess her weight.

carnival knowledge *n.* Latin phrase meaning to have sex. As in 'Have you had carnival knowledge with your wife within the last two weeks?'

carn yakunt *phr.* Coined by the *Farkarwy* tribe of Tasmania. As in 'Carn yakunt, where the Farkarwy?'

carpenter's dream *n*. Sexually promiscuous woman. As in 'Flat as a board, easy to screw'.

carpet muncher *n*. One who scoffs *hairy pie*, usually a female.

Casanova's rubber sock *n*. Condom; blob; French letter.

cathedral *sim*. Describes an oversized vagina. To the owner, one could remark 'By goodness! My organ's never played in a cathedral this size before.'

chapel hat pegs *sim*. Describes large, erect nipples. As in 'Phoarr! She had nipples like chapel hat pegs'. Also *pygmies' cocks*; scammel wheel nuts.

chase the cotton mouse, to *v*. *To have the painters in*; have flags out; surf the crimson wave.

cheeky crocodile eyes *phr*. The view of the licker from the angle of the lickee as the licker descends into the undergrowth. As in 'He/she went down to telephone my stomach with the cutest cheeky crocodile eyes. It was love.'

cheese and kisses *rhym. slang* Missus; better half; ball and chain. See also *minister of war*.

cheesy wheelbarrow *n*. The penis as it might appear while being pushed by an uphill gardener.

chicken man with ball tits *Aborig.*
Mythical dreamtime aboriginal figure who got the rainbow
serpent's daughter *up the duff* and was punished by having
his balls repositioned on his tits. Sightings generally
concurrent with *hops hunger*.

chicken man with ball tits *Aborig.* Mythical dreamtime aboriginal figure who got the rainbow serpent's daughter *up the duff* and was punished by having his balls repositioned on his tits. Sightings generally concurrent with *hops hunger*.

Chinese singing lesson, to take a *v.* To have a much-needed piss.

chin splash *n.* Condition caused by trying on a pearl necklace that is too big.

chocolate cha-cha *n.* Roof-top dance in the style of Dick Van Dyke, but performed by chimney sweeps of the chocolate variety.

chocolate iceberg *n.* Giant turd sitting in the trap, the tip of which protrudes above water level.

chocolate shark *n.* Unlike its relative, the brown trout, the appearance of this giant beast from the bumhole often causes panic among toilet-goers.

chocolate shark angler *n.* Fisherman who sails his skin boat up the cocoa canal.

chocolate starfish *n.* *Rusty sheriff's badge*; Vegemite bullet hole.

choke *n.* Controlling valve regulating pressure in the Dutch oven or botty bugle. A companion may quip, 'A bit more choke and you would have started'. See other automotive parts: *headlamps, spoilers, sixth gearstick*.

choke the chook, to *v.* Bash the bishop; burp the worm. See also *devil's handshake*.

CHOP *acronym* Chauvinistic hedonistic opportunistic prick.

chuckin' a Bradbury *v.* 1. To slip it in by slipping over. 2. To win against all logic. 3. To exhibit dumb luck. Compare *square root*.

chuckin' a Dokic *v.* 1. To object to the price of salmon at a major tennis event. 2. To eat significant amounts of garlic, raw onion and pickled or devilled eggs, then scream loudly at your offspring from the bar. 3. To unleash wild behaviour. See also *berko*.

chuckin' a Skasey *v.* 1. To piss off to a non-extraditing Spanish island, after losing billions in shareholders' money. 2. To make a miraculous recovery. 3. To need a wheelchair to drink champagne.

chuck your muck, to *v.* To drain one's spuds; ejaculate.

chuckin' a Dokic *v.*

1. To object to the price of salmon at a major tennis event.
2. To eat significant amounts of garlic, raw onion and pickled or devilled eggs, then scream loudly at your offspring from the bar.
3. To unleash wild behaviour. See also *berko*.

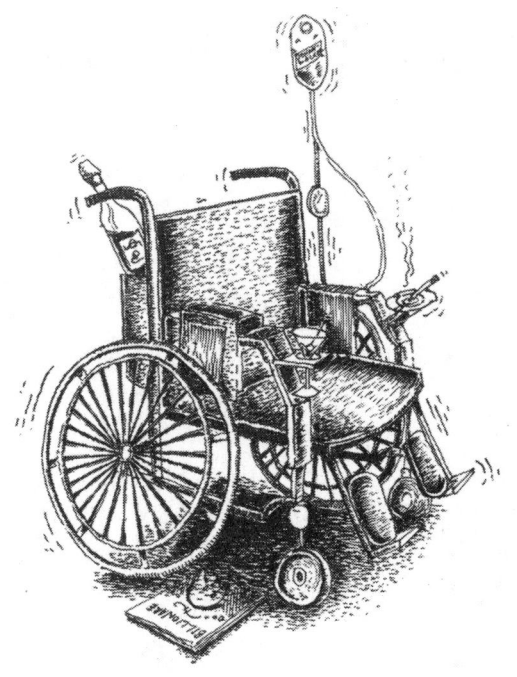

chuckin' a Skasey *v.*

1. To piss off to a non-extraditing Spanish island, after losing billions in shareholders' money. 2. To make a miraculous recovery. 3. To need a wheelchair to drink champagne.

chuffdruff *n.* Those residual flakes of manfat and fanny batter found upon the *mapatasi*. Pubic equivalent of mammary dandruff. See also *clitty litter*.

chutney locker *n.* Rectum; date locker.

clam jousting *n.* A sexual encounter between lesbians. Also known as Velcro fastening.

close combat sock *n.* Rubber; one-piece overcoat; pipe pullover; tail sheath. See also *sleeping bag for mice*.

cloud of shit, a *Brunn. n.* Fart; blow off.

clusterfuck *n.* A regrettable situation of immense idiocy.

cock-a-doodle-poo *phr.* The stooling hour. To be woken by the touching of cloth. As in 'Strange, I seem to have a cock-a-doodle-poo and a *dawn horn*. I don't know whether to push or pull.'

cock block *n.* Bed. As in 'I wouldn't mind lying *that* on me cock block'.

cock know-how *n.* Knowledge of how to please a man sexually (From *Portnoy's Complaint*). 'Boy can she suck! What cock know-how!' See also *head, good*.

cock snot *n.* Semen. As in 'Copy of *Penthouse*, please… oh, and a box of tissues. I think my cock has a cold coming on.'

cock tease *n.* Woman who wears 'fuck me shoes' and then changes into 'fuck off slippers' when you get back to her place.

cod cove See *hairy pie*.

colliwobbles *n.* **1.** A case of bad nerves. **2.** A choker who cannot cross the final hurdle. Derived from the Melbourne-based Collingwood Football Club, who made it to 14 grand finals in 50 years, but won only one.

comet vomit *n.* Powerfully projected *sidewalk signature*. Compare *get out and walk*.

conga line of suck holes *phr.* Lathamism circa 2003 about the Coalition front bench.

costume drama *n.* The frantic behaviour of a woman who cannot decide what to wear for a party. See also *period drama*. Generally advisable never to say yes when asked 'Does my bum look big in this?'

cough cabbage water, to *v.* To ejaculate; tread on the gloy bottle.

council worker *n.* **1.** Someone or something that is only half involved. **2.** A semi. See also *lazy lob on*.

court Madam Knuckle, to *v.* To light the candle, open a bottle of wine and present some flowers to Madam Knuckle and her five daughters. See *Madam Palm*.

cowboy walk *n.* Broad, rolling gait required when walking to the bog with the *turtle's head* exposed.

crack haunter *n.* He who fired his Colt six-shooter of love into the *rusty sheriff's badge*.

crack one though the covers, to *phr.* From cricketing parlance. To pitch a tent in bed. As in 'Look love, I have cracked one through the covers. Wanna face a few balls?'

crap on, to *v.* To talk excessively. Implies that words tumble like chocolate monsters from the melon of the talker.

craptacular *adj.* A stunning example of bad taste; the pinnacle of kitsch. From *Lady Bothroy's Guide to Australian Living 1876*.

crash the yoghurt truck, to *v.* Accident at the *Billy Mill roundabout*; empty the wank tanks; discharge the *trouser mauser*.

cream biscuit *n.* A satisfied post-coital vagina. See also *bulldog chewing oats*.

crock *n.* 1. A load of bullshit; a joke; a rip-off; not worth it. 2. A large reptile that eats backpackers.

crusties *n.* Overworn knickers lacking in 'April freshness'; panties with a dirty drip-tray and dusted with clitty litter.

cumofsomeyoungguy *n.* Favourite Chinese meal for men who insist on dusting curtains. Berley used by *poo-pipe pirates* from *bomb bay*.

cunt *n.* The female genitals. Once common parlance, the term has been considered impolite since the end of the 14th century. Not recommended for use in front of the mother-in-law.

cunt bubble *n.* An air-lock up the fanny, often leading to a minge burp.

Cunter Valley *n.* The fertile winegrowing region of Tasmania.

cunt-struck *adj.* Cock-happy; cunny haunted. Compare *brain cramp*.

cunt with eyes *n.* Female equivalent of a dickhead.

Cupid's toothpaste *n.* Cross between *Aphrodite's Evostick* and denture glue; that which women spit or *swallow*. Also tapioca toothpaste.

curbside crocodile *n.* Speed trap; a police car lying low in the grass or hidden behind a building to trap speeders.

curry puncher *n.* Subcontinental inspector of manholes. A wristy bowler from the *paddo end* who likes to hide and seek the curried sausage. May follow the Vegemite index on the Mumbai bourse.

curtain drop *n.* Labia length; size of a woman's beef curtains. As in 'Excuse me love, I'm doing a bit of measuring up. What's the drop of your curtains?'

curry puncher *n*. Subcontinental
inspector of manholes. A wristy bowler from the *paddo end* who
likes to hide and seek the curried sausage. May follow the
Vegemite index on the Mumbai bourse.

cut lunch, to *v.* To steal a target of affection from another. As in 'Wazza is spewin' 'cause Bazza cut his lunch. Reckons he'll go him wif a chainsaw.'

Cyclops *n.* Fabled one-eyed trouser god who vomits when he is pleased.

Dd

Entries

beginning with the above letter or character

dag *n*. Australian term of endearment. Silly nong; foolish but loveable *git*; hopeless but harmless twit.

dance with the captain, to *v*. Specifically the hand jive, Roman helmet rumba, Bologna bop or five-knuckle shuffle.

Darwin stubbie *n*. Angry blood sausage; north-pointing sloop.

daub the brush, to *v*. To *dip your wick*; do dirty work at the crossroads; pole varnishing.

David Boon *n*. The man by which all Australians measure their commitment to drinking beer. See also *52 not out*.

dawn horn *n*. Early morning tent pole; bed flute on which 'Reveille' is played; to awake with a Jake. Sometimes appearing after breakfast, at the bus stop for example. See also *big cock day*.

dead heat in a zeppelin race *phr*. Refers to large tits; knockers; bazookas; big pair of Bristol Cities; *Gert Stonkers*.

deadset *adj*. Certain. As in 'Would I shit you? Serious! Deadset!' or 'He's a deadset homo.'

Delhi belly *n*. Delicate stomach condition leading to the Brad Pitts, Eartha Kitts and red ring.

Desmond *n.* The number four. As in Desmond 2 2.

devil's handshake *n.* Reflects Catholic attitude towards masturbation.

die in a woman's lap, to *v.* Number threes, not ones or twos; to blow your load.

dildo *n.* Practice version of the pork sword.

dingleberry grove *n.* The part of the human body located between the sex organs and the anus; the perineum. So named because the coarse pubic hairs that grow in this area tend to collect dung pollen much like fruit growing on a bush. Also commonly known as biffin bridge.

dingo *phr.* Situation in which you awake with your arm under someone you met the previous evening in the throes of a *hops hunger* while wearing *beer goggles*, who is so *fugly* you would, if you could, chew your arm off rather than wake 'it'. Compare *whole lotta Rosie*.

dingo's breakfast *n.* No food, just a yawn, a piss and a good look around.

dinkum *adj.* Proud to ejaculate as an Australian.

dip your wick, to *v.* To hide the sausage; bury the salami; introduce the captain to his pie.

dirtbox *n.* Rectum; *date locker*.

dishonourable discharge *n.* The shameful result of bashing the bishop.

docker's thumbs *sim.* Large, erect nipples; *chapel hat pegs*; Scammel wheel nuts. As in 'She had nipples like a docker's thumbs'. See also *pygmies' cocks*.

dog eggs *n.* Dog turd, often 'laid' on the pavement. Also *barkers' eggs*.

dog's eye *rhym. slang* Meat pie. As in 'Get us a dog's eye, will ya? With some dead 'orse!'

dogs' match *n.* A sexual encounter in a public place. In bushes, doorways, under lamp posts.

dog with two dicks *sim.* Randy; horny. As in 'He came out of prison like a dog with two dicks'. Also tom cat with three balls.

donkey kisser *n.* She who does not kiss well; girl who kisses like a donkey chewing an apple.

donkey punch *n.* Knocking your partner out cold while approaching the *Billy Mill roundabout* from *Bourneville Boulevard*. This is said to have the same aphrodisiacal effect as slamming a goose's neck in a drawer whilst committing bestiality. Don't try either.

don't give a *phr.* Usually a toss. Others include a peppered shit; a ten-arsed goat, a blistered cat. To not care.

doormat basher
See *carpet muncher*.

double bass

double bass *n.* 1. The back passage of a large woman. Unlike the typical bum trumpet, this instrument can only produce a deeper, low-resonating note. See also *big in the shitter*. 2. Sexual position where the man enters from behind and tunes in Tokyo while flicking the wail switch.

Dracula's tea bags *n.* Tampons; jamrags; cotton mice.

dragstrip *n.* 1. A thin, highly groomed strip of vaginal hair. 2. The act of shedding clothes by those in drag.

draw mud from the well, to *v.* To *follow through*.

drink link *n.* The ATM. The crucial link between drinker and drink.

drink on a stick *n.* Erection, alluding to lollipops and oral sex. As in 'Hoy pet, fancy a drink on a stick?'

drive-by shooting *v.* The act of hitting a low note on the bum trumpet only to keep walking.

droob *n.* A cross between a dill, dork, *dag*, wimp and a drongo. From Sir Les Patterson.

drop anchor in bum bay, to *v.* To arrive at the *rear admiral's* favourite port of call.

dropkick *n.* 1. A loser; dickhead; twat; dork; tosser. 2. The way to win a game of rugby when in front of the posts with 30 seconds to go and 30 metres out.

dunny budgie *n.*

1. A large, maggot-laden fly common in summer.

2. A stockman's parrot.

drop the kids off at the pool, to *v.* To pass a stool.

drop the shopping, to See *drop the kids off at the pool*.

dry-docked *adj.* Lack of lubrication situation where a low tide of love juices prevents the skin boat sailing into tuna town.

duel with the pink Darth Vader, to See *Hand Solo*.

dumplings on that, look at the *phr.* Common inter-male mammarial observation.

dung funnel See *fudge tunnel*.

dunny budgie *n.* 1. A large, maggot-laden fly common in summer.
2. A stockman's parrot.

dunny rat, cunning as a *phr.* Unscrupulously cunning.

dunny, the great Aussie *n.* Toilet; thunderbox; Chamber of Commerce; used beer department. Traditionally located outside, over a pit. Also a popular nickname for someone called Dunn.

dunny, the great Aussie *n.*

Toilet; thunderbox; Chamber of Commerce; used beer department. Traditionally located outside, over a pit. Also a popular nickname for someone called Dunn.

Ee

Entries

beginning with the above
letter or character

eat breakfast backwards, to *v.* To throw up.

eating out *n.* Fanny lapping; muff diving. As in 'One *hairy pie* to eat in, and hold the mayo'.

Eddie McGuire *golf term* To always be in the middle, giving everyone the shits.

egg bound *adj.* Blocked of fudge pipe; constipated.

elbow bender *n.* Nudger of the turps; sauceaholic.

empty the anaconda, to *v.* To *siphon the python*.

ESD *acronym* Eat Shitty Dick. To smoke a pink cigar fresh from cack canyon. Can be used as an insult in the suggestive form, e.g. 'ESD, fuckface'.

exercise the ferret, to *v.* To copulate; bury the bishop (as opposed to bashing him).

exhaust pipe *n.* Bumhole; *fudge tunnel*. Also tailpipe.

expresshole *n.* That *dropkick* with a trolley full of stuff who snakes into the '8 items or less' checkout at Coles.

extras *n.* The tugging as opposed to the rubbing in a rub-a-tug shop.

Ff

Entries

beginning with the above letter or character

face like a basset hound licking piss off a calf's balls *sim.* Not particularly attractive.

fagla *n.* An even bigger fag.

fair suck of the sav *phr.* An expression of exasperation, used in the same way as a 'fair go, mate'.

fairy hammock *n.* Panties.

falling-down juice *n.* Beer. Also *fighting water*.

family jewels *n.* Knackers; male genitalia.

fanny bomb *n.* Moment of sexual fulfilment in a woman; female orgasm. As in 'I think the fanny bomb just went off'.

fanny fright *n.* Nervous condition affecting some macho men who suddenly become reluctant to have sex when presented with an opportunity.

fanny rat *n.* 1. Penis. 2. Sexually promiscuous male; dickwit.

Farkarwy *n.* Mythical lost Aboriginal tribe that has come to represent the state of being unaware of one's location. As in 'We're the Farkarwy?'

farnication *n.* 1. Sex while listening to John Farnham. 2. Whispering Jack off.

fart catcher *n.* Male homosexual.

fart higher than your arse, to *v. French* To harbour an inflated opinion of oneself. As in 'Zat garcon Daa-veed Beck-am. He farts higher zan eez own arse.'

fart knocker *n.* 1. Bum bandit; fudge nudger. 2. One who criticises another's farts.

fauxmosexual *n.* 1. Metrosexual; a gentlemen who looks like he prefers to sneak his meat in through the back door, but in reality dines in tuna town.

feague *v.* The equestrian tradition of shoving a stick of ginger up a horse's dock for reasons best known to those who do it. Usefully adapts to 'feague off'.

feather-bed soldier *n.* He for whom belly bumping is the be all and end all. See also *Captain Stabbin'*; *town rake*.

feature *v.* To shag; get next to. As in 'Phoar! I wouldn't mind featuring with him/her'.

feed the ducks, to *v.* To wank. From an apparent similarity in the hand movement involved.

felch *v.* 1. Californian craze of training a hamster or similar animal to jump through a *ring* on command. 2. Any other real or imagined homosexual practice, such as licking lemon curd out of a tea towel holder, or playing pass the chocolate log.

fellationship *n.* The tender relationship between members of the clergy and their young male flock.

fidiot *n.* A fucking idiot.

fighting water *n.* See *falling-down juice*.

FIGJAM *acronym* Fuck I'm Good, Just Ask Me. Compare *on-me-ism*.

filmmunoefficiency *n.* Timing your entrance to a movie so that you miss all the bullshit ads about crap to do with some shite about product victims and their new cars.

fish supper *euph. Carnival knowledge* to which a husband is entitled at the end of the day. See also *get up them stairs*.

fist rape *n.* Taking advantage of your fist after inviting it back to your place for a coffee and a flick through a dirty magazine. See also *glaze a knuckle*.

five against one *phr.* Masturbation. As in 'But mum, I never had a chance, it was five against one'. See also *shake hands with the unemployed*.

five-finger spread *n.* Highly counterproductive attempt to suppress a vomit with the hand.

fizzing at the bung hole *v.* Implies sexual arousal in a woman. 'Was she hot or was she not!? Fizzing at the bung hole, she was.' Predominantly male usage, funnily enough.

flatulence *n.* Wind; the whole business of farting. From the Latin *flatus* meaning 'smelly solo' and *lentus* meaning 'trouser trumpet'.

flesh wallet *n. Hairy chequebook*; pubic purse.

flogging on *v.* To connect to the infilthmation highway for a spot of keyboard spraying.

floppy red cup *n.* See *hairy goblet*.

follow through *v.* To accidentally soil one's underpants whilst attempting to fart; create russet gusset; drop a pebble.

foreplay *n.* 1. A misrepresentation about oneself made during a conversation aimed at eventually procuring sex. 2. Phonetic suburban Melbourne spelling for foreplay, as in 'Kim, me and Kel enjoy foreploy before sex. Fancy a Jarra?'

forget-me-nots *n.* The final notes in a *Chinese singing lesson*; droplets that form a tiny but embarrassing wet patch on your trousers. Also dicksplash.

French *n.* Popular coital position whereby the man sits astride a bicycle selling onions while the woman perches on the handlebars and inflates his testicles.

Freudian slip *n*. Something comfortable into which *Spurt Newton* slips before sex.

frig *v*. To wank or fuck, usually about.

frigmarole *n*. 1. Unnecessarily long foreplay. 2. Something that is unAustralian. From the Latin *frigus* meaning to fuck about.

fruit fly *n*. One who buzzes around fruitcakes.

fuck 1. *v*. To have it off; shag. 2. *v*. To break; damage something beyond repair. 3. *v*. To dismiss with contempt. e.g. 'Fuck that for a game of soldiers'. 4. *interj*. Exclamation of surprise or disappointment.

fucker *n*. An individual; person. Often prefixed 'big, fat'. Advisable not to prefix with 'cunt' as that may be a compliment.

fuck-in-law *n*. Womb buddy; someone who's fucked someone you've fucked. As in 'I might have a few celebrity fucks-in-law, but I'm no star-fucker'.

fuck stick *n*. Penis.

fudge packer *n*. One who packs fudge.

fudge tunnel *n*. 1. A tunnel made out of, or for the underground transportation of, fudge. 2. An arsehole.

fugly *adj*. Fucking ugly.

Gg

Entries
beginning with the above letter or character

gagging for it *v*. What people are thought to be when viewed through *beer goggles* of higher magnification. Also known as choking for it.

galloping knob rot *n*. VD; any painful social disease resulting in the production of gleet and the pissing of razor blades.

galloping the lizard *n*. Frenzied use of the wanking spanners to take the pant piston into sixth gear. Also known as galloping the maggot.

gammon flaps *n*. 1. Hole in a farmhouse door through which pigs come and go at will. 2. Beef curtains. Also known as gammon goalposts.

gangbang *n*. A bike ride on which a group of males share one bicycle.

gap lapper *n*. She who keeps short nails; a gully yodeller; a vagitarian; a Leswegian; a doormat basher. See also *carpet muncher*.

gates of gammon See *saddlebags*.

gay *adj*. Limp of wrist; tending to ask others to shut doors; critical of the 'dust in here'.

GBH *acronym* Grievous Beer Harm, usually conducted on oneself.

genital floss *n*. G-string; banana hammock.

genitalia failure *n*. The suffering of loose sausage meat; *brewer's droop*; marshmallowing of the love muscle.

Gert Stonkers See *gonzagas*.

get it on, to *v*. To get off, get it up and get your oats.

get off at Redfern station, to *v*. Coitus interruptus; withdrawal before ejaculation. Redfern is the last station before Sydney's Central Station.

get out and walk See *bushman's hanky*.

get up them stairs *v*. The cry from a chauvinist male to his wife which indicates that he has finished eating, drinking and watching the AFL and now wishes to retire to the bedroom to make an ungainly and flatulent attempt at sexual intercourse.

get wood, to *v*. The opposite of getting loose sausage meat. Also known as getting string; gibbon gristle.

giggle stick *n*. Penis; heat-seeking moisture missile.

git *n*. *Bastard*; twat. Often applied to children, prefixed 'You cheeky little' and accompanied by a swipe to the back of the head.

give Eddie a rub down, to *v.* Celebrity slaphead wanking terminology. See also *take Captain Picard to warp speed*; *Spurt Newton*.

glaze a knuckle, to *v.* To wank.

golden shower *n.* A vile sex act; an unfortunate mix-up in a crowded German bathroom.

gonad glue *n.* Gloy; *Aphrodite's Evostick*.

gonzagas *n.* See *guns of Navarone*.

goog, as full as a *phr.* Drunk or at least bloated with drink. From the northern Australian slang for egg.

goo gun *n.* Your pocket paste dispenser; jizz stick.

Gorbechev, the *n.* A popular dick-snot painting. Inspired by the shape of the birthmark of the Russian leader of the same name.

Gosford skirt, a *n.* Sydney parlance for a short skirt, i.e. just below The Entrance. This is not to be confused with an Avoca skirt, which is situated just above The Entrance and is illegal in public places.

Gough *n.* A proud, boring, arrogant cough that lasts for 3 years.

great Australian bite *n.* Going down on a solid plate of Aussie surf and turf. Usually accompanied by *cheeky crocodile eyes*.

greyhound *n.* A very short skirt, barely an inch from the hare. See also *Gosford skirt*.

grinning like a shot fox *sim.* Smug. As in 'He's just back from drinking in the *Barossa Valley*, and he's grinning like a shot fox'.

groaner *n.* A turd so big that it cannot be expelled without vocal assistance.

growl at the badger, to *v.* To noisily scoff the *hairy pie*.

grundies *rhym. slang* A Reg Grundy production. Underdaks; undies.

guard's van *n.* Of pulling a train, the least desirable position in the queue. As in 'Bags not in the guard's van, fellas'. The last gangbangster on the bike.

guns of Navarone *n.* Whoppers; tits; large breasts.

gusset grenade *n.* Fanny fart.

gusset typist *n.* A woman who wanks. Also gusset pianist. As in 'I've heard she plays the gusset piano'.

gutful of piss *n.* A skinful. See also *worm wearing sunnies*.

gutted rabbit See *mapatasi*.

Hh

Entries

beginning with the above
letter or character

haddock pie *n.*
See *hairy chequebook*.

hag *n.* Ugly woman; boiler; boot; steg; swamp donkey.

hairy chequebook
See *hairy cup*.

hairy cup See *hairy donut*.

hairy donut See *hairy lasso*.

hairy goblet *n.* Ceremonial love chalice referred to in the popular chat-up line 'Let me lead you to the altar of desire, and there I shall drink the juice of love from your hairy goblet'. Works every time.

hairy lasso See *hairy pants*.

hairy pants See *hairy pie*.

hairy pie *n.* Kipper; Velcro triangle.

half leapfrog *n.*
Sex doggy-style.

hamburger *n.* Of the female anatomy, that which can be seen in a *hamburger shot*.

hamburger shot *n.* A rear view in a pornographic magazine from which the *curtain drop* can be estimated.

ham-fisted *adj.* In the act of wanking. As in 'His mum came in and caught him ham-fisted'.

ham howitzer *n.* A military field weapon descended from the *lamb cannon*.

handbrake *n. Minister of war*, the missus; the other 'alf.

Hand Solo *n.* An intergalactic *hand shandy*.

head on him/her

hand shandy *n.* A frothy one, pulled off the wrist.

hand to gland combat *n.* Vigorous masturbation. Brutal combat involving *five against one*.

happy lamp *n. Sixth gearstick.* As in, 'I'm horny. Think I'll give my happy lamp a quick buff.'

happytitis n. A disease brought on by the consumption of vitamin VB.

have the painters in, to *v.* To menstruate; to be on the blob during rag week.

head *n.* Something which is given by women to men, and is afterwards described as 'good' by the recipient when talking to friends.

head, good *n.* Skilful blowing of the *goo gun*. See also *ridgy-didge*.

headlamps *n.* Nipples. Come in Berlin; tune in Tokyo; *baby's dinners*. See also *docker's thumbs*.

head like a robber's dog, to have a *phr.* To be *fugly*.

head like the north end of a southbound cow, to have a *phr.* Even uglier; butt ugly.

head on him/her *phr.* Prefixes exaggerated description of how ugly a person is. As in 'He had a head on him like a fricasseed trout and she had a head like a canoe full of snot'. See also *head like a robber's dog*.

heave a Havana, to *v.* To grow a tail; take a dump; unveil a bum cigar.

helicopters, attack of the *n.* Drunken rolling of the head; a sudden reminder that you need to make an urgent call on the big white telephone. See talking on the *big white telephone*.

hide the salami *n.* A bedtime game for two players, incorporating a sausage and a *hairy pie*. Also sink the salami; bury the bratwurst.

Hinch *n.* A bearded hunch proved correct.

hipocrocadogapig *n.* The ultimate unattractive female; swamp donkey; steg.

hissing Sid *n.* The name of the *one-eyed trouser snake*.

hogans *n. US* Charlies; *Gert Stonkers*; Norma Snockers.

hole *n.* Ring, quoit; hoop.

homosexual *n.* A man or woman sexually attracted to members of his or her own sex. Often in Sydney. (From the Greek *homos ecsuralos* meaning 'lifter of shirts'.)

hops hunger *n.* The desire for beer; to really seriously want a beer. Can leave you blinder than *a worm wearing sunnies*.

horizontal jogging *n.* Heterosexual sexual intercourse.

horizontally accessible *adj.* Describes someone who is always up for it; *town rake*; *yo-yo knickers*.

horn *n.* Ceremonial symbol of a man's affection for a woman, traditionally given by the woman to the man. As in 'Jeez, you gimme the horn, love'.

horse's head, to sit on a *v.* Of queues for the toilet, a more extreme case of the *turtle's head*. As in 'Hurry up will you, I'm sitting on a horse's head out here'.

hot fish yoghurt *n.* Cream sauce filling for *hairy pie*.

hot meat injection *n.* Similar to meat injection, but hot; *love torpedo*.

Howard, the *n.* A unique brand of exercise bike that comes in classic '50s design and can only be pedalled backwards. As in 'I spend fifteen minutes a day on the Howard and my calves are fantastic'.

how's your father *euph.* Sex. Often prefixed with 'ahem'. As in 'Fancy a quick bit of… ahem… how's your father?'

humdinger *n.* A real beauty; corker; bottler. As in 'She was an absolute humdinger, she was'.

hung like an Arab stallion *adj.* Donkey-rigged; well endowed. See also *basket for days*.

hungry arse *n.* Condition afflicting women in tight jeans whereby a crease in their pants seems to disappear up the crack of their arse. Compare *camel's foot*.

Hunter Valley red *n.* A sip from the crimson goblet. A tongue lashing given to her while *the painters are in*. The Hunter Valley red is generally considered inferior to the *Barossa Valley* due to its proximity to Newcastle and rusty aftertaste.

hurl *v.* To hoy (up); call Huey.

Ii

Entries
beginning with the above
letter or character

IBM

IBM *acronym* 1. Itty Bitty Meat. A small penis. 2. Inches Below Muff. The units in which a skirt is measured.

I can't believe it's not batter *phr.* Possible advertising slogan for KY Jelly.

ICBM *acronym* Of modern-day, state-of-the-art trouser weaponry, Inter Cuntinental Ballistic Missile.

ignisecond *n.* That overlapping moment of time when the hand is locking the car door even as the brain is saying, 'Shit, my keys are inside!'

I'm with Ansett *phr.* Ironic statement, meaning absolutely not, out of the question. Said with heavy sarcasm.

in like Flynn *phr.* Mimicking the general ability of noted Australian actor, Errol Flynn, to find his way through most doors of a woman's property.

intestinal tourist *n.* Passport-holding backtracker.

Jj

Entries

beginning with the above letter or character

jamboree bags *n.* Funbags.

Jana Wendt, to *phr.* To get the fuck out of there; when one gets up and goes, one just Wendt.

jerk the gherkin, to *v.* To burp the worm; jerk off; *crash the yoghurt truck* into *Madam Palm and her five sisters*. See also *throttle Buddha*.

jerkle *n.* A circle of worm burpers. A conference of hand shandies.

Jesus Christ, a *v.* To come back from the dead and crack another; get back on the beer horse; have the hair of the dog.

jiggle the jewellery, to See *jerk the gherkin*.

jill off, to *v.* Female equivalent of jack off; to paddle the pink canoe. Until it leaks.

Johnsing *n.* Realising you don't really live in a cemetery.

jerk the gherkin, to *v.*

To burp the worm; jerk off; *crash the yoghurt truck* into *Madam Palm and her five sisters*. See also *throttle Buddha*.

Kk

Entries

beginning with the above
letter or character

kahoonas (ka-*hooo*-naaaz) *n.* Large, wobbly breasts; golden bodangers; kermungers; *Gert Stonkers*.

kangaroo shagging a spacehopper, like a *sim.* Energetic sex or a promiscuous woman. As in 'Bloody hell! I bet she goes like a kangaroo shagging a spacehopper.' Also like a shithouse door in the wind.

kelpie *n.* Culinary seaweed that tastes suspiciously like dog.

Ken Oath *phr.* The Australian saint of all things definite.

Khyber *rhym. slang* Arse. From Khyber Pass.

kidney wiper *n.* Slat rattler. See also *purple-headed womb broom*.

kiss the porcelain god, to *v.* To talk on the *big white telephone*.

kitten hammock *n.* Bra.

kitten's noses *n.* Nipples.

Kling-ons *n.* 1. Winnets; *dingleberries*; anal hangers-on. 2. One of numerous races of Star Trek alien with bumpy foreheads.

knee trembler *n.* Intercourse while both parties are standing up. Often in a shop doorway.

knockers *n.* 1. Breasts. As in 'What a lovely pair of knockers'. 2. Of football punditry, those who have criticised a player in the past. As in 'Well, Brian, the lad has certainly had his knockers'.

Ll

Entries

beginning with the above letter or character

labia lard *n*. Fanny batter.

labrador lipstick *n*. Stalk; erection.

lamb cannon *n*. An arms development dating back to somewhere between the *mutton musket* and the *bacon bazooka*.

lapper *n*. *Pink oboe* virtuoso; *hairy pie* eater.

last meat supper *n*. Final fling before marriage. It's all *fish suppers* thereafter.

lathered *adj*. Pissed; plastered; paralytic.

laughing gear *n*. The mouth, used for talking. As in 'I called a guy a cuntfucker one time … then I realised it was sort of a compliment, so we had a bit of a laugh and then he punched me in my laughing gear.'

launch your lunch, to *v*. To laugh liquidly.

lavatory *n*. Smallest room; little house; loo; water closet; convenience; place of easement; shithouse; crapper; privy; bog; latrine; cackatorium; temple of cloacina; toilet; kharzi; thunder box; comfort station; dunny.

lavender *n*. Male homosexual.

lay a cable, to *v*. To *build a log cabin*; grow a tail; drop a copper bolt.

lay of the land

lay of the land, the *phr.* A term of prestige awarded to women with impressive *cock know-how*.

lazy lob on *n.* Semi-erect penis; dobber. See also *council worker*.

lead in your pencil, to have *v.* To be with big beef olive rather than loose sausage meat.

lesbo See *lezzo*.

let off, to *v.* To fart; blow off; launch an *air biscuit*.

let one go, to *v.* To pre-plan the release of a fart into the wild.

let Percy in the playpen, to *v.* To consent to intercourse; allow Percy into the tunnel for a shunt.

let rip, to *v.* To fart; blast off.

lettuce licker *n.* Lesbian; bean flicker; tuppence licker.

lezzo *n.* A serf of Baron von Munchausen. See also *carpet muncher*.

lezzo boots *n.* Any clumpy, unfeminine footwear worn by women. The opposite of fuck me shoes.

lickalotopus *n.* Scientific name for a bean licker of prehistoric reptilian proportions.

lick both sides of the stamp, to *v.* To drive on both sides of the road; travel on both buses; be AC/DC.

lifting the cheek *n.* The sly behaviour of a cushion creeper.

like Whitney dressed as Britney *phr.* An older woman making every effort to recapture her younger days, often failing.

lip reading *n.* The observation of women in tight pants who have a *camel's foot*. As in 'If she bends over any more, I'll be able to read her lips from here'.

lip ring *n.* A lipstick line around the pork sword showing how far it has been swallowed.

liquid laughter *n. Puke; psychedelic yodelling.*

little death *n. French* In a male, the post-bonk feeling of shagged-outity.

live in the pavilion, to *v.* Intensifier of *to run in from the pavilion end*. As in 'He doesn't run in from the pavilion end, mate. That one *lives* in the fucking pavilion.'

Liverbong *n.* Situated on the ocean side of the colon. Like a billabong, it only fills up when it's pissing down.

log jam *n.* A skin flute conference in the *laughing gear*. Ironically, the log jam makes it very hard to laugh.

long-distance call *n.* STD; venereal disease; the clap. As in 'Poor bloke got a long-distance call from London'.

love puff *n.* Gentle *air biscuit* launched in the direction of your partner in bed, often the morning after a curry, in an attempt to cement the intimacy of the moment.

love socket *n.* Vagina; entry point for the main cable. Also known as rocket socket, *serpent socket*, spam socket.

love torpedo *n.* Penis. As in 'I sank her bacon battleship with my purple, hot love torpedo'.

lower than shark shit *phr.* A very unfavourable observation on the quality of an individual.

lunch at the Lazy Y, to *v.* To dine out cowboy style, on *hairy pie*, beans and coffee.

lunchbox lancer *n.* Archaic mediaeval term for a cocoa shunter. First used by King Arthur to describe the French army. In 562 AD he wrote: 'Fear not the French, for their knights are without heart, and their King without wisdom. But keep thine backs as to the wall, for amongst their number thou shalt find more than a few lunchbox lancers, I can tell you.'

luncheon truncheon *n.* *Spam javelin.*

lung butter *n.* Phlegm; green smoking oysters. Compare *get out and walk*.

lure of the hairy magnet *phr.* The stuff of life.

Mm

Entries

beginning with the above
letter or character

McShit, to go for a *v.*
To enter a fast food outlet with no intention other than to release a few brown trouts before leaving. Compare *drive-by shooting*.

McSplurry *n.* The viscous bowel movement that follows eating at fast food restaurants.

mac in the bath *n.* English overcoat; French letter. In the same vein as *sleeping bag for mice*.

Madam Palm and her five sisters *n.* A wank. As in 'I'm nipping off to bed with Madam Palm and her five sisters'. Known also as *Palmela Handerson*.

make a bald man cry, to *v.* Masturbate. As in 'I was reading an *art pamphlet* recently, for the articles of course, and it was enough to make a bald man cry'.

Malvern Star *n.* The town bike on whom everyone's had a ride; Tardis twat.

mangina *n.* A penis so small it could be hers. See also *IBM*.

man mayonnaise *n.* Manfat; gentleman's relish.

man trap *n.* Female genitals; hairy love-pit, *one-eyed trouser snake* snare.

mapatasi *n.* (ma-pa-ta-zee) *n.* 1. Minge. As in 'Show us yer mapatasi!' 2. *abbr.* Map of Tasmania. From the similarity in shape of said island to a *muff*.

masshole *n.* A huge, huge bloody arse. Compare *whole lotta Rosie*.

meat-seeking pissile *n.* Penis; *love torpedo*; guided muscle.

Melboring *adj.* Derogatory term to describe the city of Melbourne.

Melvin *v.* To grab by the balls.

merchant (banker) *rhym. slang* Wanker.

Mick, me mate the masterfarter, *lyric* Potent or loud opening of the lunchbox, celebrated by singing the traditional bush ballad which centres on the exploits of 'Mick, the man who put the art back into farting with his double-jointed arse'. Poet laureate Kevin Bloody Wilson still lives on performance royalties from these happy events.

Mimi 1. *v.* An unconventional way of temporarily becoming as famous as a sibling. 2. *n.* A whale watcher.

minge mat *n. Mapatasi*; Velcro triangle.

minge whisker *n.* 1. Striptease artist. 2. She who flashes her gash, e.g. whilst folding her legs.

minister of war *n.*
The other half, the spouse of Sir Les Patterson.

mink *n.* A more upmarket name for the wife's *beaver*.

Montezuma's revenge *n.* A term for diarrhoea not appreciated by Mexicans; the Tijuana cha-cha.

moose *n.* An ugly woman, often a feminist with hairy armpits, who may like the taste of carpet. Boiler; steg.

moregasm *n.* Someone or something that gives you enormous pleasure.

morning glory *n.* The appearance of a tent pole first thing in the morning. See also *awaken the bacon*.

moss cottage *n.* The ideal home for John Thomas.

mouseturbate *v.* To partake in one-armed web surfing. See also *flogging on*.

Mr Happy's business suit *n.* Condom.

Mr Sausage *n.* The excitable trouser man.

Mr Whippy *n.* Flagellation; corporal punishment dished out at rug-a-tug shops.

mud *n.* Excrement.

muff 1. *n.* Minge; fanny. 2. *v.* To shag; have intercourse with. 3. *v.* To fluff (not to be confused with fluffer); miss an easy goal-scoring opportunity, e.g. 'Oh fuck! Matty Richardson has muffed it.'

muff huff *n*. Menstruation or PMT. See also *period drama*.

muffin top *n*. An unflattering item of clothing. This piece falls a little short of the belly, revealing an excess of stomach which overflows the belt-line like the excess of muffins over its wrapping.

mumbler *n*. A woman in very tight pants. You can see her lips move, but you can't quite make out what she is saying. See also *camel's foot*.

mutton musket *n*. A smaller more portable field weapon than the *lamb cannon*. Also known as mutton bayonet, mutton dagger.

mystery bus *n*. The bus that pulled in late on Saturday evening while you were in the dunny and took away all the ugly women.

mystery taxi *n*. A taxi that comes while you're still asleep to pick up the stunner you took home the previous evening and replace her with a *dingo*.

Nn

Entries

beginning with the above
letter or character

nadbag *n.* Nutsack; pod pouch; scrot sling.

nads *n.* 1. Simple way to annoy anyone called Nadine. 2. (*abbr.* gonads) Clackers; knackers; hairy conkers; marbles; *bollocks*; pods. *US* Nards.

NBR *acronym* No Beer Required. Someone you would chat up instantly as opposed to someone who requires a keg. Compare *two bagger*, *whole lotta Rosie*.

nether eye *n.* That single, unseeing eye, situated in the nether region, which cries brown, lumpy tears.

Noah *rhym. slang* Shark, from Noah's Ark.

nob *v.* To shag; poke; penetrate with the knob.

nocturnal donkey *n.* 1. A night-time beast of burden laden with *population paste*, wanting to trek the wilds of Tasmania.

nocturnal emission *n.* Doc-talk for a wet dream.

nom de tug *n.* Fake name adopted by employees of adult recreation facilities.

nookey *n.* Sex, only a bit of which is advisable to have at any one time.

norgs *n.* Fun bags; *baby's dinners*; traditional stop before ordering a *bikini burger*.

Norman *n.* 1. The act of conceding. 2. A backyard sporting concession. As in 'Carn mate, you never said over the fence was out. So go on, gimme a Norman.'

nuggets *n.* 1. Testicles. 2. Any inedible part of a chicken or turkey, coated in batter or breadcrumbs.

number one *n.* A stand up.

number two *n.* A sit down.

nunga munching *n.* The ganneting of *hairy pie*; the doing of horatio.

nut custard See *banana yoghurt*.

nuts 1. *n.* Knackers; scrotum and/or its contents, as in 'I'm going to shave my nuts'. 2. *adj.* Mad, as in 'Shave your nuts? You must be nuts.' 3. *n.* Things that monkeys eat. As in 'That monkey's nuts. I gave it some nuts and it's rubbing them on its nuts.'

nympho *n.* Sex-crazed bird that's *gagging for it* 24 hours a day, 7 days a week. The sort who would shag a pneumatic drill and blow up the generator.

Oo

Entries

beginning with the above
letter or character

ocker *n. & adj.* A person who is proudly Australian, wearing singlet, boardies and thongs. 'I'll 'ave a pinelime splice, a packa Winny blues and a meat pie fanks, luv.' Generally comes with a prolific talent for euphemisms and laconic observation.

off like a bucket of warm sick *phr.* Very, very seriously bloody off. Like really.

off your face *adj.* Shitfaced.

off your trolley *adj.* Mental; hatstand.

oil the bat, to *v.* To polish the pork sword; lubricate the *lamb cannon*.

old red wine, like an *sim.* Anyone who likes to be laid at an angle in a cellar. See also *carpenter's dream*.

one-eyed night crawler in a turtleneck sweater *n.* Pant muscle; pecker; penis.

one-eyed trouser snake *n.* Gentleman's pant python; sex serpent; cock.

one-eyed Willie *n.* Penis.

one-eyed Willie's eye patch *n.* Condom; English overcoat.

one-eyed zipper fish See *Cyclops*.

one-handed mag *n.* Jazz magazine; rhythm read; *art pamphlet*; porny periodical.

one in the departure lounge *phr.* The need to defecate. As in 'Jeez mate, I got one in the in the departure lounge. Know where the big knobs hang out?" See also *touch cloth*, *turtle's head*.

on-me-ism *n.* The lingua franca of someone fair up themselves; refers to the way the conversation is invariably directed.

open your lunchbox, to *v.* To float an *air biscuit* reminiscent of yesterday's egg sandwiches.

over the shoulder boulder holder *n.* Industrial bra; heavy lifting apparatus for jelly water mangoes.

owner-operator *n.* Wanker; a knight who wields his pork sword for pleasure, not for the benefit of fair maidens.

Pp

Entries

beginning with the above letter or character

paddo end *n.* Kak klaxon; friend of the *back door conquistador*. See also *barking spider*.

Palmela Handerson *n.* Your dream date to go out for a cruise in the wanking chariot.

park the custard, to *v.* To vomit.

park the tiger, to *v.* To *puke*; *yodel*; let out a *technicolour yawn*.

parlour *n.* Back passage. As in 'His *pork prescription* was most efficacious, taken in the parlour of course'.

passhole *n.* 1. That dickhead driving slow in the fast lane. 2. The person who drives slowly for miles but speeds up the minute you try to pass.

passion flaps *n.* A more romantic alternative to *piss flaps*.

passion pit *n.* Bed. See also fart sack, scratcher, wanking chariot.

passion wagon *n.* Clapped out van, usually a Ford Transit, with blacked out windows and a piss-stained mattress and several empty beer cans in the back. Also shag wagon.

Pavarotti *n.* 1. Well-known Italian tenor. 2. A fat lot of good. 3. A ten-inch penis. As in 'Did you see the size of the mutton dagger in *I Ream of Genie*? It was a Pavarotti and then some!' 4. A ten dollar note.

pavement pizza *n.* The contents of your stomach as they appear after *barfing* in the street; a *parked tiger*.

Pearl Harbour *phr.* A nasty nip in the air; brass-monkey weather.

pearl neck brace *n.* Voluminous pearl necklace; dick snot cast.

period drama *n.* Moody and erratic behaviour of women at times of menstruation.

personalities *n.* Breasts. As in 'My, you've got a lovely pair of personalities'. (Fnarr fnarr) See also *baby's dinners*.

phantom farter *n.* An anonymous benefactor.

pigsty *n.* A cop hangout: Maccas, Burger King. Occasionally the police station.

piker *n.* Bludger; pinko; jellyback; *council road worker*.

pilot of the chocolate runway *n.* Navigator of the windward passage.

pink cigar *n.* Penis. As in 'Tell me Madam, do you per chance smoke the pink cigar?'

pirate of men's pants *n.* Swashbuckling term for your jolly Rogerer; cock; penis.

piss *v.* To *siphon the python*; bleed the lizard; milk the taipan; void the viper; tap the tiger snake; drain the death adder; Jimmy Riddle; hi-diddle-diddle; bubble and squeak; you and me; a snake's hiss; angel's kiss; damage the Doulton; dangle the mongrel; drain the spuds; flash fanny at the Fowler; point Percy at the porcelain; splash boots.

piss flaps 1. *n.* Labia; beef curtains. 2. *interj.* Exclamation of disappointment. As in 'Oh, piss flaps! I never win on the Melbourne Cup!'

play the back nine, to *v.* To play Irish golf; use your wood to play into the bunker; get the dog in the bathtub.

play the bone-a-phone, to *v.* To wank; pull yourself a *hand shandy*; play the one-string banjo.

play the pink oboe, to *v.* To perform oral sex on a man. Often to denote homosexuality, as in 'I didn't know Molly played the pink oboe'.

play the whale, to *v.* To spew.

plumber's toolbag *n.* Furry bicycle stand; mott; *mapatasi*.

plums *n.* Knackers; balls; testicles.

pocket billiards *n.* A game for one player, two balls, and a cock.

pocket fisherman *n.* He who plays with his tackle through his trouser pockets.

polish the lighthouse, to *v.* To masturbate in the bath.

poon *n.* Fanny; crumpet; toosh. 'I guess this means my poon days are over.' (John F. Kennedy after his inauguration in Jan. 1961) 'Knickers off, this is poon city!' (Bill Clinton after his inauguration in Jan. 1993).

poop catchers *n.* Knickers; cack catchers.

poop chute *n.* Bumhole; *arse*.

poo-pipe pirate *n.* Jolly Rogerer; *pirate of men's pants*.

population paste *n.* Joy gloy; semen; spunk; *Aphrodite's Evostick*.

pork *v.* To shag. As in 'I couldn't pork her because she *had the painters in*'.

pork prescription *n.*
1. Cock, to be swallowed twice a day before meals.
2. Doctor's authorisation for a meat injection.

pornfolio *n.* A portfolio of your porn work, covering both electronic and print media. As in 'Dear Buttman, if you take a careful look at my pornfolio, you'll see I'm quite the right person to play the male lead in *Doctor Proctor*'.

porridge gun *n.* Tool for distributing *population paste* quickly and efficiently.

posh wank *n.* A mess-free masturbatory manoeuvre undertaken whilst wearing a *sleeping bag for mice*.

potty-mouth *n. US* Someone who repeats words from this book in general conversation.

premature pinch *n.* The snipping off of an unsmoked bum cigar when disturbed in the act, by a rare win from the South Sydney Rabbitohs, for example.

psychedelic yodelling *n.* Vocal projection of your *biscuits* from your mouth.

puke *v.* To throw up.

purple-headed womb broom *n.* Purple-headed yoghurt warrior.

pygmies' cocks *sim.* Erect nipples. As in 'She had nipples like pygmies' cocks'.

Qq

Entries

beginning with the above
letter or character

queef *n. US* Vaginal fart; front botty burp. Also *kweef*.

queen See *queer*.

queer See *queen*.

quickie *n.* Hurried one.

quim *n.* Refined name for the *mapatasi* such as a gentleman might use at a Camberwell cocktail party. From the Welsh word 'cwm', meaning 'valley beneath the 13 amp fuse wire'.

quince *n.* 1. Mincing quean. 2. Something owls eat with a runcible spoon.

quoit *n. Ring,* hoop; *rusty sheriff's badge*; balloon knot; tea towel holder.

quumf *v.* To sit in waiting outside a public library and sniff ladies' bicycle seats as soon as possible after their owners have dismounted and gone inside. Also to snudge.

Rr

Entries

beginning with the above letter or character

ragman's coat *n.* Unkempt pubic hair.

ralph *v.* To vomit; call Huey.

rat-arsed/faced *adj.* Shitfaced.

reach around, to *v.* In botting, to pour your partner a *hand shandy* whilst ramshackled.

rear admiral *n.* Captain of the good ship Butt, a *poo-pipe pirate*. He who steers from the stern and/or sails the windward passage.

rear gunner *n.* In aviation terms, a gunner who shoots one of his own side by firing his *lamb cannon* into their *bomb bay*.

Rex Hunt *v. & n.* To hook a person then kiss her/him goodbye in the morning; a one-night stand.

rib cushions *n.* Breasts.

ridgy-didge 1. *adj. Dinkum.* 2. *n.* Head, good, especially by those with a talent for circular breathing. Playing the ridgy-didge is generally a better experience for all than playing the didgeridoo. See also *nunga munching*.

ring *n.* 1. *Hole*; jacksie; anus; brown eye; *chocolate starfish*. 2. Vagina.

ring bandit *n.* A *Vegemite driller*; Tontine biter.

ringkerchief *n.* The ritual cloth used by arse bandits to clean the *paddo end* after *dropping anchor in bum bay*.

ring stinger *n. Rear gunner; back door conquistador.* See also *sneaky butcher*.

ripper *adj.* Excellent; no worries. Antonym: *Barry Crocker*.

road train *n.* A line-up of bodies in a gangbang. As in 'Then I ran my *trouser mauser* head-on into a road train like I played for Canterbury Bankstown'. See also *bulldoggin'*.

rob the date locker, to *v.* To turd burgle.

rock and roll *rhym. slang* Dole or welfare. A regular Arts grant.

rocket polisher *n.* Over-enthusiastic cleaning of the *meat-seeking pissile*, leading to detonation on the launch pad.

rodeo sex *n.* Doggy-style sex during which you call your girlfriend by an ex-girlfriend's name, and then try to hold on for as long as possible. Also bronco sex.

roe boat *n.* Rags; manhole cover; pleasure garden padlock; red flag.

roger *v.* To shag, often in the past tense. As in 'I gave her a jolly good rogering'.

Ronny Coote *rhym. slang* Root. As in 'Did ya Ron 'er, mate?'

root *v.* To embrace without trousers.

root, the feeling of *n.* A quasi-spiritual state related to the Australian male's innate 'sixth sense of hornbag', as described by philosopher Rodney Rude in his seminal text, *Rude Rides Again*. 'The feeling of root hangs heaviest in the air in summer.'

root ute *n.* The high-octane temple of belly bumping.

rough as guts *phr.* Colourful phrase calling attention to someone's state of being, usually the morning after a *hops hunger*.

Rumpleforeskin *n.* Penis; Fagan; John Thomas; junior. See also *stubby holder*.

rusty box *n.* A woman sporting a red minge.

rusty sheriff's badge *n.* Ride along biffin bridge from *Slim Dusty's hairy saddlebags* and there it lies, right in the middle of cack canyon. Just before you reach rump gully.

Ss

Entries

beginning with the above letter or character

saddlebags *n.* 1. Labia; *piss flaps*. 2. Scrotum. Also *Slim Dusty's hairy saddlebags*.

salad dodger *n.* Fat bastard. As in 'Jeez, don't that Rivkin and Richardson make a pair of total salad dodgers!'

salmon canyon *n.* Piscine pass leading to tuna town that some folks round these parts call gobblers gulch.

Samsonite basher *n.* Australian commercial traveller, coined by Sir Les Patterson.

sausage basting *n.* Shagging.

SBD *acronym* Of farts and farting, silent but deadly. A subtle release of pungent botty gas. Compare *drive-by shooting*.

schload *n.* A large quantity; a lot; a shitload.

scrote *n.* Knacker; bollock brain. A versatile testicular term of abuse.

scrotum *golf term* Two balls next to each other on the fairway.

seagull *n.* The arching G-string revealed when a woman bends over to pick up the shopping.

see you next Tuesday *acronym* Parting nicety alluding to the initials 'CU' N.T.

semi *n.* 1. *Lazy lob on*; half-erect penis. As in 'The best I could manage was a semi'. 2. A house joined to another house.

send a sausage to the seaside, to *v.* To dump; sink a few U boats.

septic tank *rhym. slang* Yank. Also refers to the unrelenting septic that passes for North American TV entertainment.

serpent socket *n.* The hole with which the *one-eyed trouser snake* connects.

sexile *n.* The state of living involuntarily in a world without sex; rootless. As in 'Jeez, poor Macca's been in sexile for a whole year!'

shag slab *n.* The altar of love; bed; passion pit; *cock block*; fart sack; scratcher.

shake hands with the unemployed, to *v.* To bludgeon the beefsteak; buff the banana; *make the bald man cry*. See also *box the Jesuit*.

shat on from a height, to be *v.* To be badly exploited; humiliated; let down.

shave a horse, to *v.* To have a piss; take a leak.

shaven haven *n.* A de-bearded clam; bald monkey's forehead.

Shazza *v.* To have sex with several filthy tramps on a piss-stained mattress, all at once.

sheep shagger *n.* 1. Anyone with a New Zealand passport. 2. A 'bro'.

shit-eating grin *n.* Exaggerated, smug, self-satisfied smile pulled deliberately to taunt others; as if to say 'Eat shit'.

shit on your own doorstep, to *phr.* To foul the nest. For example, to shag your mother-in-law while you are totally pissed.

shits, the *n.* Of smallroom dancing, those up-tempo trots which include the Tijuana cha-cha, the sour apple quickstep and the Aztec two-step.

shit yeah *exclam.* Absolutely! Antonym: *I'm with Ansett*.

shonky *adj.* Dodgy; dubious.

shoulder boulders *n.* Big breasts; *gazungas*.

shrimp on the barbie, to chuck another *phr.* Seppo scorching. To burn an American for everything they've got.

Sicilian commerce *n.* Ordering a Venetian chandelier from your cousin Roberto who owns a lighting warehouse and imports from the old country who says he can also arrange delivery 'cause his sister's husband Tony has an uncle whose mate, Angelo, has a truck and also a mate whose neighbour is an electrician who owes him a favour and will do it for cash. Capice?'

sidewalk barking *n.* The act of vomiting; *technicolour yawning*; talking to the gutter; chatting to the plumbing; driving the porcelain bus.

sidewalk signature *n*. *Liquid laugh*; *hurl*; hork; spew; *ralph*. See also *sidewalk barking*.

siphon the python, to *v*. To point *Percy* at the porcelain; have a piss.

sixth gearstick *n*. Elusive G spot referred to in mythical sexual texts, the search for which is considered unAustralian.

slabicide *n*. The act of drinking a slab by yourself. Compare *52 not out*.

slap the monkey, to *v*. To burp the worm.

slash *n*. *Piss*; wee wee.

slash and burn *n*. 1. Third world deforestation technique. 2. A painful symptom of venereal disease.

slash palace *n*. Public lavatory.

sleep in a tent, to *v*. To have a large penis. As in 'Fancy coming back to my place? You'll not be disappointed. I sleep in a tent.'

sleeping bag for mice *n*. Sprog sheath; condom. See also *Casanova's rubber sock*.

sleeping beast *n*. Flaccid cock; marshmallowed main pipe.

Slim Dusty's hairy saddlebags *n*. 1. Gammon gates; beef curtains; *piss flaps*. 2. Furry beanbags; yoghurt industrial complex; testicles.

slip her a crippler, to *v*. A few notches up from *slip her a length*; to shag someone so hard they can't walk.

slip her a length, to *v.* To shag, from the male viewpoint. As in 'I'd slip *her* a length any day of the week'.

Slum Disty *n.* A poverty-line, dyslexic country musician.

slurder *v.* To murder a slab. See also *slabicide*.

smurfing *n.* One-armed web surfing. See *mouseturbate*.

snake charmer *n.* A girl who has an uplifting effect on your pant python. As in 'Phoar! She's a bit of a snake charmer. I'm pitching a trouser tent right here and now.'

snatch mouse *n.* Tampon. Also cotton mouse.

sneaky butcher *n.* He who is always trying to sneak the meat in through the back door. A *poo-pipe pirate* who likes to dock his good ship Percy in bum bay.

snookered behind the red *phr.* Unable to sink the pink due to the time of month. The only pot on is a difficult brown.

snorker *n.* Australian for sausage, both eating and hiding varieties.

snowdropper *n.* Underwear fetishist who steals to sniff, usually from washing lines.

snufty *n.* One who derives pleasure from sniffing bicycle seats, drip trays, socks.

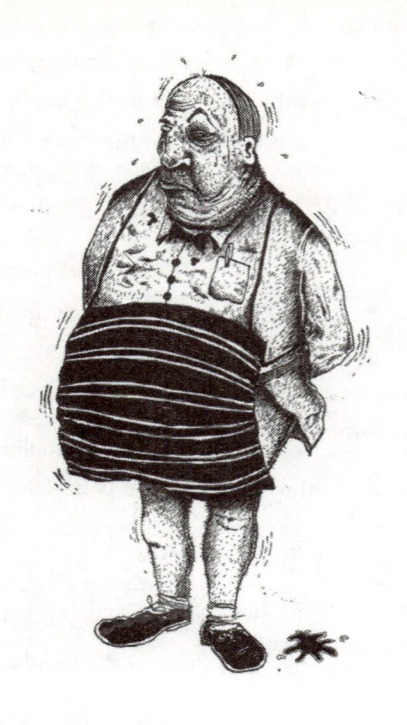

sneaky butcher *n.*

He who is always trying to sneak the meat in through the back door. A *poo-pipe pirate* who likes to dock his good ship Percy in bum bay.

soap-on-a-roper *n.* Heterosexual male who prefers not to bend down in communal showers.

sook *n.* Whingeing tosser; girl's dick.

sour puss *n.* Foul smelling cock box; stench trench.

spadger *n.* Vagina.

Spam alley *n.* A haven for *Spam javelin* throwing.

Spam castanets *n.* Labia. As in 'My hobbies include playing the Spam castanets.'

Spam javelin *n.* Penis.

Spam sceptre *n.* Largest of the *family jewels*.

spank the monkey, to *v.* To spank the plank; splatter the cheese platter.

speedball *n.* Clitoris; mound in the *Red Centre*; tongue punch bag; budgie's tongue. Not far from *Alice Springs*. Also man in a boat.

sperm wail *n.* The verbal ejaculation emitted during the male orgasm.

sperm worm *n.* Penis.

spider's legs *n.* Of *muffs*, rogue pubic hairs that protrude beyond the knicker-line; a pant moustache.

splashback *n.* Unfortunate tidal effect of a depth charge or *belly flopper* within the pan, resulting in splashing of the arse.

spoilers *n.* Buttocks.

spoof *n.* Sperm that's only fit for parody.

Spurt Newton *n.* The balletic crescendo involving the pork piccolo in the second act of Swine Lake. Pet name for the tearful bald man sitting on the hairy beanbags. See also *die in a woman's lap*.

spurt your curd, to *v.* To spread your spunk; infect others with your pluck and spirit.

square root, a *n.* Sex that one gets despite prevailing maths.

stalk fever *n.* Condition affecting men on *big cock day*.

step on a duck, to *v.* To create a quack; fart. *orig.* From a remark made by King Edward VI upon hearing a hunting companion sound his trouser trumpet: 'Sir, I may be mistaken, but I do believe you have stepped on a duck'.

step on a frog, to *v.* Also tread on a frog. See *step on a duck*.

stiffy stocking *n.* Rascal wrapper; cheesepipe cling film; *Spurt Newton's* sickbag.

Sting *n.* 1. Really crap English singer who makes a living promoting Tantric sex and boring the pants off *Bugle* readers. 2. Cack-pipe stabbing. See also *baloney colonic*.

stinky finger *n.* The result of having eaten the captain's pie without a knife and fork.

stir the porridge, to *v.* To have sloppy seconds.

stubby *n.* A semi. See also *council worker*.

stubby holder *n.* 1. Uncircumcised penis; helmet pelmet. 2. State of semi-arousal. To put a throwdown in the stubby holder is to have a semi. 3. Front-bum, fur-burger, gash.

stuffing a marshmallow in a piggy bank, like *sim.* Of those unfortunate situations involving brewer's droop, attempting to force your loose sausage meat into the slot.

stupicide *n.* An act or instance of unintentionally killing oneself due to the state of being stupid, dense, dumb, obtuse or thick.

surfboard *n.* Flat-chested female; not Elle Macpherson.

swallow *v.* What women do when they don't spit; what Goldilocks did to one of the three bears' porridge.

switch hitter *n. US* 1. Person who bats with both hands. 2. A bisexual; AC/DC.

sword swallower *n.* Sword as in the pork variety.

Tt

Entries beginning with the above letter or character

tadpole net *n*. Blob; rubber Johnny; cheesepipe cling film.

tail ender *n*. Small dollop of doo that you must wait for after the main stool has been expelled. The final roof detail to be applied when *building a log cabin*.

tail gunner See *rear gunner*.

take Captain Picard to warp speed, to *v*. *TV baldy/cock euph*. To masturbate; strangle Kojak.

talk a glass eye to sleep, s/he could *phr*. Will not shut the fuck up; *could talk under wet concrete*.

talk under wet concrete, s/he could See *talk a glass eye to sleep*.

tanked up 1. *adj*. Arseholed. 2. *Military* Being sufficiently equipped with tanks. 3. *Vet*. A pet shop with an aquatic emphasis.

tap, to be on the *v*. To be on the piss.

tap off, to *v*. To successfully *tap up*.

tap up, to *v*. To chat up; try to instigate a sexual liaison.

Tasmaniac *n*. A dribbling, stuttering mess whose eyes are too close together.

technicolour yawn *n*. A *pavement pizza*.

thong *n.* 1. An informal form of footwear much loved by Australians. Not allowed in casinos or revolving restaurants. 2. A skimpy alternative to the full brief; anal floss; t-bar.

throttle Buddha, to *v.* To inaugurate the Right Honorable Member for Underpants; tug the boat; spray the *population paste*. See also *jerk the gherkin*.

thunder bags *n.* Underpants; trollies. See also *grundies*.

Titanic *n.* A date who goes down the first time out.

toey *adj.* Gaggin' for it. As in 'He's as toey as a Roman sandal'.

toilet sausage *n.* Brown-eyed mullet. See also *Bondi cigar*.

Tony Blair *n.* Governor of the 51st state of America.

touch cloth, to *v.* To be at the stooling stage. That awkward moment immediately after the *turtle's head* pops out of the *dung funnel* and rattles the cloth cage. Leaves owner of said arse with *cowboy walk*.

town rake *n.* Swordsman, stud. He who has cleaned up the town.

trough lolly *n.* Toilet candy.

trouser mauser *n.* The Right Honourable Member for Underpants.

trouser waltz *n*. Post-beverage, pre-coital ritual performed in the dark and in the presence of a semi-conscious partner. From Sir Les Patterson.

truffle hunting *n*. *Growling at the badger*; giving face; telephoning the stomach; eating tuna taco. Usually accompanied by *cheeky crocodile eyes*.

turtle's head *n*. The initial flanging of the stool. The moment when the turtle sees the light at the end of the dung tunnel. Go to the light, little turtle, go to the light.

two bagger *n*. Someone so ugly you need two bags, one for them and one for you in case theirs falls off. Usually results in a *dingo*.

two-pot screamer *n*. Someone with a low tolerance for alcohol; easily intoxicated; a cheap drunk.

Uu

Entries

beginning with the above letter or character

up to the apricots

UDI *n.* Unidentified drinking injury. A mysterious injury received during a *bender*, of which the victim has no recollection.

Uluru *n.* Mound in the red centre; lab kebab; vertical bacon sandwich; fur burger, adjacent to *Alice Springs*. Docking bay for the *womb broom*. See also *gammon flaps*.

umecarparknow *phr.* Pronounced 'U-me-car-park-now'. A traditional Australian male term used to convey to another male the desire to further discuss a contentious point in the pub car park ASAP. Often occurs in concert with *berko* or *chuckin' a Dokic*.

umfriend *n.* A concealed intimate relationship. As in 'This is Sue, my… um, friend'.

Umglish *n.* Form of language spoken by stoners. As in 'Umm errrr ahhh… can ya roll us another, Wayne?' 'Jah mahn.'

unlateral thinking *n.* To think about being inside the box. Brings on *brain cramp*.

upchuck *v.* To chuck up. As in 'Oi, did ya see Chuck upchuck?'

up periscope *n.* Bathtime game for up to one person.

up the duff *adj.* In the pudding club; with a bun in the oven.

up to the apricots *phr.* Sir Les Patterson's true measurement of affection.

Vv

Entries

beginning with the above
letter or character

vagina *n*. Alcove; bat cave; bear trap; *bearded clam*; bearded taco; beaver; bermuda triangle; box; bucket seat; cake; chuff box; cockpit; cooch; coochie; coochie-pop; coose; cooter; cooze; crack; crawl space; cum dumpster; cuntcake; *cunt*; cunny; donut; dripping delta; felted mound; fillet-o-fish; finger hut; fish; fish taco; front bum; fly catcher; fuckhole; furburger; garage; gash; gates of heaven; golden doorway; Grand Canyon; growler; *hair pie*; hatchet wound; heaven's door; hole; honey cave; honey pot; hot box; jaws of hell; lobster pot; loins; loose meat sandwich; lotus; love box; love canal; lower lips; meat wallet; muff; nooch; nook; nookie; parking spot; peach; pearly panty gates; pocket; *poon*; poontang; purse; pussy; quiff; *quim*; rat trap; scratch; sheath; slash; slit; snapper; snatch; space; split; stench trench; tampon socket; temple; thingy; tool shed; tuna; tunnel; twat; undercut; vertical smile; wishing well; whisker box; womb; x; *yoni*.

Vanstoned *adj*. Having escaped from a country where your wife served as a sexual slave of the royal family and its zoo animals only to end up living upon the guano of Nauru.

Vegemite driller *n*. Workman on the Vegemite motorway.

Vegemite motorway *n.* Anus; *arse*; back passage; the final frontier. Haunt of *brown-pipe engineers* and *poo-pipe pirates* running behind the wind.

Vegemite stripe *n.* Brown stain or skidmark found on unwashed *grundies*.

vinegar strokes *n.* Of males on the job, the final climactic stages of intercourse or masturbation. As in 'Would you believe it? The phone rang just as I was getting onto the vinegar strokes.' From the similar facial expression associated with sipping vinegar.

vixen *n.* Wily bird; young temptress; foxy chick. E.g. Stevie Nicks circa 1978.

VPL *n.* Visible Panty Line.

vurp *n.* A burp which brings up a foul-tasting quantity of stomach contents small enough to be gulped straight back down again.

Ww

Entries
beginning with the above
letter or character

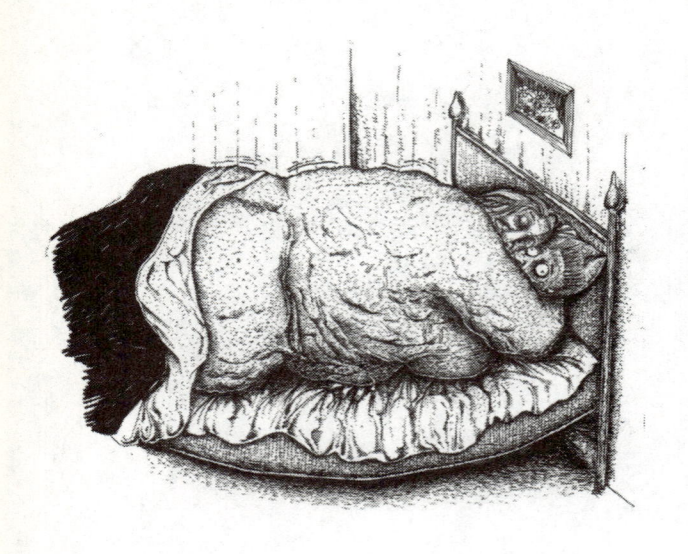

whole lotta Rosie *n.*

Sex/wrestling position named by (original and only) AC/DC singer Bon Scott in which a heavy woman pins scrawnier prey and has her way with him, regardless of his feelings on the matter. Compare *two bagger*.

Wagga Wagga *n.* 1. An Italian with a stutter. 2. A bush cricket umpire from NSW with no fingers or tongue.

wankerchief *n.* Spoof rag.

welcome mat *n.* Trail of fine pubic hair rising majestically from the *mapatasi*.

whack-fart 1. Complete idiot; moron; no hoper; cross between whacker and wanker. 2. An inappropriate fart, e.g. during sex, dinner party or funeral eulogy.

wheelchair weed *n.* Strong marijuana, serious shit. Leaves smoker babbling in *Umglish*.

white pointer *n.* Topless sunbather.

whole lotta Rosie *n.* Sex/wrestling position named by (original and only) AC/DC singer Bon Scott in which a heavy woman pins scrawnier prey and has her way with him, regardless of his feelings on the matter. Compare *two bagger*.

wide on, a *n.* Female hard on. Generally after the partner puts on the fish mitten or pulls into *cod cove*. Heralded by *labia lard*.

windsock *n.* Uncircumcised penis. See also *stubby holder*.

wobbly boot on, he's got the *phr.* He's had a few.

wombat *n.* Eats, roots and leaves. See also *dingo's breakfast*.

work bench *n.* The altar of love; bed; *cock block*; where Percy shunts.

worm wearing sunnies, like a *sim*.
Blind drunk; blotto; pissed as; flogged; maggoted;
shitfaced; off one's nut; plastered. As in 'Big night, mate?'
'Fuckin' oath mate, I was like a worm wearin' sunnies!'
Generally follows a *hops hunger*.

Xx

Entries
beginning with the above
letter or character

XXX

XXX *adj.* Obscene.

XXXX *adj.*
Even more obscene.

XXXXX *adj.* Unspeakable.

Yy

Entries

beginning with the above letter or character

yabbie *n.* Young Australian Boring Businessperson; coined by Sir Les Patterson.

yinyang 1. *n. US* Arse; bum. 2. Fuckwit; dupe.

yodel See *york*.

yodel in the canyon/valley, to *v.* See *growl at the badger*.

yongles *n. US* Testicles.

yoni *n. Ancient Hindu* Female genitals; fanny.

yonks! *exclam.* Popular vocal reaction to finding a tenner on a cartoon pavement.

york *v.* To vomit. Also call Huey.

yo-yo knickers *n.* Bike; loose woman; woman whose knickers go up and down faster than the Aussie dollar.

you can't make raspberry jam from sheep shit *phr.* No, you can't.

Zz

Entries

beginning with the above
letter or character

zaftig

zaftig *adj.* Juicy. Ideal comedic alliterating adjective to prefix *zeps*.

zeps *n. abbr.* Zeppelins. Large breasts. Also Hindenburgs.

zig-a-zig ahhhh! *echoism* To have a bloody good wank watching a Spice Girls video.

zinzanbrook (zin-zan-*bruck*) *NZ rhym. slang* Fuck.

zipper fish *n.* Penis; trouser trout; underpant eel.

zipper sniffer *n.* Hunter of the pant python, male or female.

zonked *adj.* Pissed; wankered; wazzed.

zoob/zubrick *n.* Penis.

zook *n.* Prostitute.

Zorba *n.* Sex in the Greek style. As in 'Sorry Terry, my arse is red raw. Zorba is out tonight.'

zounds *exclam.* God's wounds. 17th century swear word banned by act of parliament in 1651, but okay now if used in moderation. Also gadzooks.

zucchini *n. US* Penis.

zuffle *v.* To wipe your cock on the curtain after having sex, usually in a posh bird's house.

No.s

Entries beginning with the above letter or character

100 grand scratchy, like a *sim*. To intensely stimulate the clitoris. As in 'I was rubbing at *Uluru* like a 100 grand scratchy'.

2.30 *n*. Chinese dentist time. As in 'Harrow, you cum see me for frilling at Tooth Hurty?'

404 *n*. One who is clueless. Originating from the World Wide Web error message, '404. Not found'. See also *fidiot*.

52 not out *phr*. A phrase of encouragement to a lagging mate. Refers to nuggetty Tasmanian opener David Boon's monumental effort on a flight from Oz to England in 1989 during which he downed 52 beers. Other cricketing stats of import include Don Bradman's 99.94, Matthew Hayden's 380 and Courtney Walsh's 519.

Acknowledgment bit

Big up to genius and inspiration of Viz's *Roger's Profanisaurus*, ewes guys rok! Other contributors were Scotty 'da Man' Davis from Key Biscayne, Peter Barnet, Charles Cuninghame, Lenny Hyatt, Seldon Hunt, Steven 'Mulla' Gray, Dan Austin, Simon Wooldridge and Andrew White.